HOCKEY

PLAY THE GAME

HOCKEY

CARL WARD

BLANDFORD

First published in Great Britain in 1989
by Ward Lock. This revised edition published
by Blandford, Villiers House, 41/47 Strand
London WC2N 5JE
A Cassell Imprint

Reprinted 1994 (twice)

Designed by Anita Ruddell

Illustrations by Bob Williams

Text set in Helvetica
by Litho Link Ltd, Welshpool, Powys, Wales
Printed and bound in Great Britain by
The Bath Press, Avon

British Library Cataloguing in Publication Data

Ward, Carl
    Hockey. – (Play the game).
    1. Hockey, – Manuals
    I. Title   II. Series
    796.35′5

    ISBN 0 7137 2445-5

Acknowledgments

The author and publishers wish to thank the
following for kindly supplying the pictures in
this book: Allsport (pages 26/7 – Chris Raphael
– and page 65 – Simon Brutt); Colorsport
(pages 30/1, 39, 50/1, 58, 79), Sporting Pictures
(UK) Ltd (pages 2, 11 and 39) and *Hockey
Field* Magazine (page 73), and also the Hockey
Association for their assistance in the revisions.

Frontispiece: **Sean Kerly of England and Great
Britain. For many years one of the most feared
and respected strikers in the world.**

CONTENTS

FOREWORD

I was very pleased to accept the publisher's invitation to write a foreword to this publication. The author, Carl Ward, has been able to draw from his vast experience of teaching, playing and coaching in all levels of the game in his preparation of this book, which is orientated primarily at the beginner.

After a brief history of the game, the reader is guided through the pitch markings, equipment and generally accepted hockey terminology, which is useful for players, teachers and coaches, alike, who are embarking on hockey for the first time.

The guidance and advice given on the techniques and tactics of the game are clearly written and emphasize the simplicity with which these areas can be approached. It is the measure of a high-quality educationalist that a complex situation can be taken and the factors involved prioritized such that the less experienced performer and coach are able to grasp the principal issues and gain immediate rewards through their success. The Rules Clinic is an excellent way for both players and officials to learn more about the umpiring of the game, as the situations bring the Rule Book to life.

This book is clearly written by a player and coach with the young player in mind, and I am certain that both the players themselves and their coaches will gain a great deal from the information and knowledge given in the text and diagrams.

This publication is an important addition to any hockey library, and we at The Hockey Association are grateful to Carl Ward for the time he has given to writing *Play the Game: Hockey*.

David Whitaker O.B.E.,
Coach to Great Britain

HISTORY &

DEVELOPMENT OF

HOCKEY

Hookie, hawkey, horkey or hockey – so called because of the hook of the stick with which it is played – is of considerable antiquity and like many other sports can trace its origin to early civilizations. Hockey historians have discovered strong evidence to show that some form of the game was played by the Egyptians 4,000 years ago and by the Greeks 2,000 years ago.

The Romans developed the game from the Egyptians and the Greeks and passed it on to the European nations they conquered. The German game of *Kolbe* and the Dutch game of *Het Kolven* (a forerunner of ice hockey) may have been direct descendants of the Roman game, as, probably, was the French game of *Hocquet*. Many people believe that it is from the word *hocquet*, meaning shepherd's crook, that the word hockey was derived. Other historians have looked to link hockey with hurling, the Irish game, which claims to be the oldest organized stick and ball game.

No matter what they were called, the old games of *hocquet*, hockey, hurling, shinty and bandy all had certain things in common – the size and shape of the sticks used, and

the fact that they were rough, dangerous games with few rules, if any.

From these roots there developed two vigorous branches of the sport, one quiet and scientific, the other rowdy and active: one in which the sides contended alternately and drove the ball round a specific course, the other in which they strove simultaneously to keep the ball moving forwards and backwards within certain limits. One developed into golf, the other into hockey.

The absence of rules in a game played with sticks by rowdy, energetic participants led, inevitably, to accidents and injuries, some serious. Demands for a set of rules to be drawn up grew steadily stronger until in 1868 the Eton College Chronicle attempted to do just that.

These, it is generally believed, were the first set of hockey rules ever to be written down, and they bear a remarkable similarity to some of the rules that govern the game today. For example, teams were restricted to eleven a side and included a form of goalkeeper. Goals could only be scored from within a specified area and the game was started by a 'bully-off'. Amazingly, despite this attempt to regularize the game during the nineteenth century, it still remained a very casual and disorganized activity. Nevertheless, the game was beginning to catch on and gained in popularity, particularly in the English Public Schools. Sports clubs, such as Blackheath, who already had strong connections with golf and football, began to play the game. The influence, in those early days, that one 'organized' sport had on another still generates much discussion and debate. Three things are, however, well known. First, that hockey teams at Blackheath and other 'union' clubs were made up of fifteen players. Secondly, this was the beginning of 'union' hockey, a game not played with a ball, but with a 'bung' or cube of solid rubber, and, thirdly, that during this time the game grew, changed and became more popular, spreading eventually as far as Bristol where, in 1887 at the Imperial Hotel, Clifton, a meeting of the representatives from local clubs was held and the National Hockey Union was formed.

At about the same time, another group of sportsmen, the cricketers from Teddington, were developing and introducing their own form of hockey to the region. The main difference between their game and the one played by Blackheath and the members of the National Hockey Union was that the players at Teddington used a ball not a bung. This produced a much faster, free-flowing game, where passing and stickwork flourished and the hacking, sticking, scrummaging and chaos of the game played with a bung became things of the past. Pitch markings and patterns of play similar to soccer began to be used while method and order was introduced into the 'new' game. Once the shooting circle was introduced, modern hockey was born.

The players from Teddington introduced their new game to neighbouring clubs and it was from this network that the first Hockey Association was formed in 1875. Despite this the game struggled to acquire stability and an identity. The main reason appears to have been the variation in rules adopted by individual clubs.

So it was, in 1886, that another significant meeting was held, this time at the Holborn Restaurant in London where, having agreed the rules of the game, the members turned their attention to the rules governing the Hockey Association. Once both of these were firmly established, hockey began to flourish and spread. The enthusiasm for the game was not confined to the borders of England and records show that the Irish, Welsh and Scots all adopted the game with relish. It was, in fact, the Irish and Welsh who first played an international hockey match, at Rhyl in 1895. The Irish won 3-0. Three months later the English invited the Irish to play them at Richmond and won 5-0. This was England's first ever international hockey match.

It was about this time that the first known ladies' hockey club, Molesley, was formed. Its proud record began in 1887, with Ealing and Wimbledon being formed shortly after. It is also known that the students at Lady Margaret Hall and Somerville College, Oxford were playing hockey in the 1880s and that by 1890 the game had spread to Newnham College, Cambridge. But there was still no co-ordinating body for women's hockey.

Meanwhile, in Ireland, as with the men, the popularity of the women's game led to the formation of the Irish Ladies' Hockey Union, the first national association for women's hockey. The place was Dublin, the year 1894. That year also saw the first visit of a ladies' hockey team from England – made up of students and ex-students from Newnham College, Cambridge – to Ireland, to play Alexandra College, Dublin. Having tasted international hockey the players returned, enthused and motivated to play more international matches and determined to form a national association.

The Irish were invited to play England at Brighton the following year (1895). The match ended in a goalless draw but this did nothing to dampen the enthusiasm of those committed to the furtherance of the game. Fresh from the match, five determined ladies met in a Brighton tea shop and decided that a Ladies' Hockey Association should be formed and that the rules of the Hockey Association should be adopted. This informal meeting, in April 1895, preceded the first formal meeting of the Ladies' Hockey Association which took place on 23 November 1895 in Westminster Town Hall.

One of the new association's earliest decisions was to seek affiliation to the newly formed Men's Hockey Association, a move that obviously caused alarm in male circles for it provoked the Hockey Association to state rather bluntly that it 'could not officially recognize the existence of the new association'. Determined not to let this caustic rebuff stand in their way, the Ladies' Hockey Association decided to go it alone and although they continued to play to the men's rules of the game many other changes were to take place in the next ten

years. The first, in 1896, was the change in title to the now-familiar All England Women's Hockey Association. Then followed much debate about matters concerning competition dress, publicity, public antagonism and general approval for the game.

Despite all this, the women's association and the game blossomed, developed and spread at a remarkable rate. The game seemed to symbolize the new spirit of emancipation of the age, and through it the lady players were able to assert their spirit and individuality.

There followed a period of consolidation. The need for tough pioneering, hardship and indignities faded away and was replaced by an era of opportunity for all those women who wanted to play. The five territorial associations were established. Regular international matches were played against Ireland, Scotland and Wales, while enterprising tours were undertaken to New Zealand, Australia, South Africa and the USA where the game was now being played.

HOCKEY

Similar developments were taking place in the men's game where the colonial globe-trotting of the British people, and particularly the British Army, helped to introduce and establish the game in various countries all over the world. Nowhere was the impact of the game's introduction to be felt more emphatically than in India, where in 1895 the Calcutta Hockey Club was formed. By the time of the 1928 Olympics the Indians had added a new dimension and a whole new array of skills to the game and took the Olympic title for the first time. They continued to dominate the event for the next five Olympics until their reign was ended by the Pakistani team in 1960.

Great Britain's challenge for Olympic honours did not come until 1948 when on entering the competition for the first time they won the silver medal. Great Britain's absence from the Olympics was a direct result of its decision not to become part of the sport's new international ruling body, the International Hockey Federation (FIH). This had been established to ensure the sport's inclusion in the Olympic movement. Hockey had been left out of the 1924 Paris Olympics, and this prompted a Frenchman, Paul Leutey, to set up the FIH.

Strangely, it was the formation of the Women's International Hockey Federation (IFWHA) which was proving to be the stumbling block to women's hockey being admitted to the Olympics, and at one point there were even two women's World Cups being staged – one by the FIH, which now had a significant women's membership, and one by the IFWHA.

Holland won the first FIH title in 1974 in France, while England took the IFWHA World Cup in Edinburgh in 1975. By 1979 the IFWHA had been absorbed by the FIH. The women's game was finally admitted into the Olympics in 1980.

The Olympics remained the only major international tournament until 1962 but world hockey was changing and the demand for other competitions was increasing. The 1970s saw the introduction of World and European tournaments for men and women. Junior (Under 21) events followed. It was not long before Club Championships and Champion's Trophies were included as well as international competitions for indoor hockey. Many argued that the congestion would threaten the stability and future of the game. Thankfully this has not proved to be the case and the game has gone from strength to strength with many league and cup competitions being introduced at local and national level in order to determine the qualifiers for national and international competition throughout the world.

It is now readily recognized that increasingly higher levels of competitiveness and the advent of synthetic grass surfaces have combined to push hockey into the limelight of world sport. In the British Isles this advancement has been reflected in a succession of medal-winning performances by both men's and women's teams, culminating in the ultimate accolade for the game – the winning of the Olympic Gold Medal by the Great Britain men's team in Seoul in September 1988.

Stefan Blocher who was one of West Germany's outstanding players.

EQUIPMENT & TERMINOLOGY

The pitch

Hockey can be played on either natural grass or artificially constructed surfaces. The field of play is rectangular and is 100yd (90m) long and 60yd (55m) wide. Its boundaries must always be clearly marked out with lines in accordance with the plan opposite.

The longer lines are called the side-lines, and the shorter lines the back-lines. That part of the back-line between the goal posts is called the goal-line.

A centre-line 50yd (45m) from the back-lines and two 25yd (22m) lines are marked across the field.

To assist in the control of the 'hit-in' from the side-lines, a line 2yd (1.8m) in length is marked across the centre-line and the 25yd (22m) lines. This mark should be drawn 5yd (4.5m) away from, and run parallel to, the outer edge of the side-lines.

A mark of 12in (30cm) in length must be placed inside the field of play on each side-line and parallel to the back-line, and 16yd (14.5m) from its inner edge.

To assist in the taking of penalty-corner hits, there should always be a mark inside the field of play on the back-lines on both sides of the goal. These marks should be at 5yd (4.5m) and 10yd (9m) intervals from the outer edge of the nearer goal post. There should also be a mark for the taking of long-corner hits. This mark should be inside the field of play, on the back-line and 5yd (4.5m) from the outer edge of the side-line. All these marks must be 12in (30cm) in length.

The penalty spot, from where penalty strokes are taken, is marked in front of the centre of each goal. The spot must be 6in (15cm) in diameter and the centre of the spot must be 7yd (6.5m) from the inner edge of the goal-line.

No lines or markings other than those shown on the plan are permissible on the playing surface.

Flagposts placed at each of the four corners of the field and at the half-way line, must be between 4–5ft (1.2–1.5m) in length. They should be positioned as shown in the diagram opposite.

The goals

The goals are always situated at the centre of each back-line. They consist of two perpendicular posts 4yd (3.6m) apart, joined together by a horizontal crossbar 7ft (2.1m) from the ground.

The goals must be positioned so that the front base of each goal post touches the outer edge of the back-line. The goal posts may not extend upwards beyond the crossbar, nor should the crossbar extend

EQUIPMENT · & · TERMINOLOGY

Pitch dimensions.

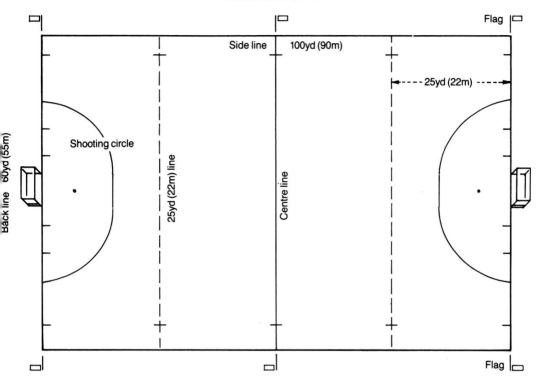

Shooting circle dimensions.

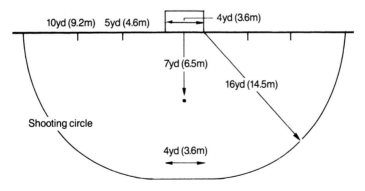

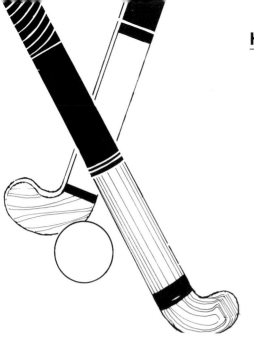

Hockey sticks and ball.

Modern hockey sticks showing the flat side, or the face of the stick, with which the ball can be played and the rounded side, or back of stick, which cannot be used to play the ball. The ball can be smooth or dimpled, as shown in the diagram.

sideways beyond the goal posts.

The goal posts and crossbar must be rectangular, and be 2in (5cm) wide, and not more than 3in (7.5cm) deep. They must be painted white.

The nets should always be firmly attached to the goal posts and the crossbar at intervals of 6in (15cm), and must also be fixed firmly to the ground behind the goal.

The backboard, which is placed at the foot of and inside the goal nets, must be 18in (45cm) in height and 4yd (3.6m) in length. The sideboards must also be 18in (45cm) high, and are required to be no less than 4ft (1.2m) in length.

In front of each goal, a semi-circle is drawn 16yd (14.5m) in radius. This incorporates a line 4yd (3.6m) long which runs parallel to, and is 16yd (14.5m) from, the back-line. This line is continued each way to

meet the back-lines by quarter circles, which have the inside front corner of the goal posts as centre. The space enclosed by these lines is known as the **shooting circle**.

The ball

The hockey ball is spherical and weighs between $5\frac{1}{2}$oz (156g) and $5\frac{3}{4}$oz (163g). The circumference of the ball must be between $8\frac{13}{16}$in (22.4cm) and $9\frac{1}{4}$in (23.5cm) approximately.

The ball must be hard – it can be hollow or solid. The outer surface can be constructed of any natural or artificial material. The surface is usually smooth, although some seams and indentations (as with a golf ball) are permitted.

The traditional colour of the ball is white, but the team captains may agree upon the use of a ball of any other colour, as long as it contrasts with the colour of the field of play.

A ball used in international matches must meet detailed standards laid down by the FIH. These cover hardness, balance, smoothness, surface, moisture absorbance, friction and bounce qualities.

The stick

A hockey stick must have a flat face on its left hand side only. The whole of the flat side, and the whole length of that part of the handle which is above the flat side, is considered to constitute the face of the stick.

The head of the stick, technically that part below the lower end of the splice, must be curved and made of wood. It is not allowed to have any edgings, insets or fittings of metal or any other substance, nor should there be any sharp edges or dangerous splinters on the stick face. The curved head of the stick must not exceed 4in (10cm). It must not be cut square, or have pointed edges. Its edges must be rounded.

A hockey stick must not exceed 28oz (793g) in weight, nor be less than 12oz

(340g). It must also be of such a width and size that it can be passed through a ring having an interior diameter of 5.1cm. Stick design, and construction, has changed dramatically over the years and at each stage has affected the style of play prevalent at the time.

The earliest stick was simply a 'weapon with a bent knob or hook at the end . . . and used for the purpose of striking the ball'. Later on, sticks were shaped from single pieces of wood, usually oak or ash, but being of one piece of wood they stung the hands when used to make long hard passes; naturally, for comfort alone, a short-passing game was developed. The flexibility and whippiness of holly changed all that and produced a long-hitting, more open pattern of play.

Later the sticks of the time, whether of oak, hickory, maple, ash or holly, began to adopt a familiar, tidy shape, and there was no restriction on length, weight or width. A wide, flat face gave more scope for stopping, dribbling and flicking – but the sting still remained.

It was in 1896 that Slazengers Ltd exhibited the first so-called spliced/glued stick, and soon sticks with cane-sectioned, cricket bat-type handles were introduced. Ash was the standard wood. The width of the stick was restricted to 2in (5cm). A common feature of all these solid 'English' sticks was the largeness of the crook. Ash was a difficult wood to fashion and bend sharply. Although suitable for flicking and pushing, the large crook made reverse-stick play difficult and restricted dribbling to a series of sharp taps on the ball.

No-one is sure how or why it happened but around 1936 the Indians developed and introduced a hockey stick with a shorter, rounder crook or head. The effect of the change was revolutionary and introduced new levels of stickwork and dexterity to the game that are emulated and practised even today.

Today's sticks have heads made of mulberry, a much harder wood which lasts much longer and can be bent more sharply. The handles are made from the best Tahiti and Manau cane, built up in sections of laminated rubber and wood, and reinforced with fibreglass, carbon fibre and Kevlar. Many sticks are manufactured to meet the specialist needs of today's top players, and modifications are continually sought and introduced to try and match the requirements of modern hockey played on the fast and consistent synthetic grass pitches.

Players' equipment

The players of the same team all wear the same colour shirt, except for the goalkeeper who must be distinctive and wear a shirt which is different to his team-mates, the opposing team and, if possible, the umpire. Players of the same team are also expected to wear identical shorts and socks. Their shirts should be numbered, often according to their position on the field:

1 – Goalkeeper
2 – Full back
3 – Full back
4 – Midfielder/defender
5 – Central defender
6 – Midfielder/defender
7 – Forward/midfielder
8 – Striker/defender
9 – Striker
10 – Striker/defender
11 – Forward/midfielder
12 + – Substitutes

Footwear varies greatly according to the surface on which the game is being played. On natural grass the players usually wear boots with nylon, rubber or moulded studs. For playing on artificial and synthetic grass surfaces players now wear multi-studded shoes. Flat non-studded shoes are favoured for indoor hockey and on some artificial pitches.

Shin- and ankle-guards are worn by all

players to protect their lower legs, while the practice of protecting hands and knuckles with tape is becoming more common. Many players also wear a gum-shield to protect their teeth and mouth from serious injury.

Goalkeeping equipment Perhaps the greatest changes and advances in recent years have been applied to goalkeeping equipment. Today's game requires the goalkeeper to wear a large range of protective equipment:

- Ice hockey style helmet
- Throat protector
- Chest pad
- Shoulder pads
- Elbow pads
- Gloves
- Abdominal protector
- Genital protector or Box
- Padded shorts
- Lightweight leg-guards
- Knee pads
- Lightweight kickers
- Boots

The position of readiness for goalkeepers.

A goalkeeper in full equipment.

This equipment is required whether playing indoors, on grass or synthetic surfaces, because the new goalkeeping techniques developed indoors and on artificial surfaces at international level are now being introduced and used at all levels and on all types of surface.

The role of the goalkeeper has changed tremendously in recent years. Good-quality equipment affords the goalkeeper the protection required and provides him/her with the confidence to utilize the entire body in exercising the skills required in a variety of situations.

The goalkeeper is now looked upon as having a more active role in his team.

TERMINOLOGY

Advantage   Umpires can allow play to continue even when an offence has been committed, if they are satisfied that by enforcing the penalty the team offended against, more often than not the team in possession of the ball, would be further disadvantaged.

Back-stick   The rounded, right-hand side of the stick which is opposite to the flat-face or left-hand side of the stick. It includes the whole of the rounded side and all of the handle above it.

Bully   To 'bully', one player from each team stands square on to each other, facing the side-lines, each with his/her own back-line to his/her right. The ball is placed on the ground between the two players and both must simultaneously tap first the ground beside the ball and then each other's stick, over the ball, three times alternately, after which they can attempt to play the ball with their sticks and put it into play.

Centre   Also known as a cross, the act of a player hitting the ball firmly towards the shooting circle from the side of the pitch.

HOCKEY

Effective use of the arms, legs and body to present as large a barrier as possible to the striker making the shot.

Circle Refers to the 'semi-circle' marked out in front of each goal; to count as a goal, a shot must be made within this circle.

Dribble The action of 'carrying' or manoeuvring the ball while keeping it in close contact with the stick. Often used to beat an opponent.

Far post The goal post furthest away from the player in possession of the ball.

Flick The flick occurs when a stationary or rolling ball is pushed and raised off the ground.

Free-hit Following an infringement, play is restarted with a free-hit to the non-offending side.

Goal-line That part of the back-line which is between the goal-posts.

Green card This is triangular in shape and shown to the players by umpires as a 'final warning' for persistent breaches of the rules and/or misconduct.

Halfway line Refers to the centre-line on the pitch which is 50yd (45m) and equidistant from each back-line.

Hit-in When the ball is put out of play over the side-line, a member of the team not responsible for putting the ball out of play is allowed to put the ball back into play with a 'hit-in', from the spot at which the ball was put out of play.

Indian dribble A method of dribbling first used by players from the Indian Sub-Continent in which the ball is tapped or dragged rapidly from left to right with the stick, in front of the player, as he/she searches for an advantage.

Intercepting   The act of seizing possession of the ball as it is passed between players of the opposing team.

Marking   When defenders keep close to players from the attacking team in order to make it difficult for them to get away or get possession of the ball.

Near post   The goal post nearest to the player in possession of the ball.

Obstruction   When a player intentionally prevents an opponent from playing the ball by interposing his/her body between the ball and opponent.

Off-side   When an attacker is in the opposing 25yd (22m) area and receives the ball from a forward pass with less than two opponents between him/her and the opposition goal-line.

Pass-back   The method of starting the game from the centre-line at the beginning of the first half and re-starting it at the beginning of the second half, or after a goal has been scored.

Penalty stroke   This is a free shot (a push, flick or scoop) at goal from the penalty spot, 7yd (6.5m) in front of the goal, awarded for infringements inside the circle.

Red card   A circular card shown by the umpire to indicate that a player has been dismissed from the field of play and permanently suspended from the game.

Reverse-stick   The use of the flat side of the hockey stick in an 'upside-down' or reversed position when playing the ball on the left side of the body. The stick is sometimes used in this position to control passes received from the right, and when passing from left to right.

HOCKEY

16-yard hit This is the equivalent of a 'goal kick' in soccer. It is awarded to the defending side after the ball has been hit over the back-line by the attacking side.

Square pass A pass made laterally across the pitch.

Striker An all-out attacking player whose job it is to score goals.

Tackle The action of a defender in trying to dispossess an opposing player of the ball.

Third-party obstruction An offence caused by a player off the ball interposing himself/herself between an opponent and the ball in a manner that allows a player from his/her own team to gain an unfair advantage.

Through pass A defence-splitting pass to an attacker running towards goal.

Yellow card The showing of a square card of this colour by the umpire to indicate that a player has been temporarily suspended from the game, usually for about five minutes.

Zonal marking A tactic used by defenders to occupy and cover areas of the pitch in order to deny the opposing team space in which to play.

THE GAME –

A GUIDE

Hockey is in many ways similar to soccer. Each team, for example, has eleven players, one of whom must be the goalkeeper. Each team is permitted to use up to two substitutes, although this is not mandatory at any level, but once a player has been substituted he/she is not allowed to re-enter the game.

The game is usually played over two periods of 35 minutes with a half-time interval of 5–10 minutes. At half-time the teams change ends.

Before the game starts, the captains of both teams meet to toss a coin. The winner of the toss has the right to choose which end his team will attack in the first half or the right to have possession of the ball at the start of the game. The captain of the opposing side will automatically have the second option.

The game is started with a pass-back from the centre of the field. The ball may be pushed or hit along the ground, but must not be raised intentionally. At the moment the pass-back is taken no player of the opposing team must be within 5yd (4.5m) of the ball and all the players of both teams, other than the player making the pass-back, must be in their own half of the field. The ball is deemed to be in play once it has been moved from its original resting place in the centre of the field.

Even the principles of play for attack and defence in hockey are similar to those of soccer, the main aim being to propel the ball into your opponents' goal. To score a goal the ball must pass wholly across the goal-line, between the goal posts and under the crossbar after having been struck or deflected by an attacker from inside the shooting circle. It is now, when we look at the rules of the game, that we begin to notice the differences between hockey and soccer.

There are eighteen principal rules of the game of hockey and they cover all aspects from the organization and conduct of the game through to procedures for re-starting a game in the event of an accident or injury to a player. For technicalities and full details of the official rules the reader is referred to the official Rule Book which is available from the Hockey Association or All England Women's Hockey Association.

The game is controlled by two umpires who administer the Rules. These umpires are the sole judges of fair and unfair play during the game. Each umpire is primarily responsible for the decisions in his/her own half of the field for the whole of the game; they do not change ends. The umpires are also responsible for keeping the time for the duration of the game.

Umpires have wide discretionary powers to penalize rough and dangerous play, time-wasting or any other behaviour which may amount to misconduct. There are ten major offences and players are not permitted to:

1 Play the ball with the rounded side or back of the stick. Only the flat side or face of the stick can be used to propel the ball.

2 Take part in or interfere with the game unless he/she has a stick in his/her hand.

3 Raise any part of the stick in a dangerous or threatening manner at any time but especially when stopping, playing or attempting to play the ball.

4 Hit the ball wildly into an opponent or play or kick the ball in a dangerous manner or in a way that is likely to lead to dangerous play.

5 Stop, play or propel the ball either on the ground or in the air with any part of the body.

6 Use the foot or leg to support the stick in order to resist the challenge or efforts of an opponent.

7 Pick up, throw, carry, kick or propel the ball in any manner except with the stick.

8 Hook, hit, hold, strike out or interfere with an opponent's stick at any time.

9 Charge, kick, shove, trip, strike at or personally handle any opponent or his/her clothing.

10 Obstruct or prevent an opponent from playing the ball by interposing the body or stick between the opponent and the ball.

Only the goalkeeper is exempted from some of these rules and is allowed to kick the ball or stop it with any part of his/her body including the hand, but only within the confines of the circle.

Hockey by its nature is a competitive game which involves a good deal of stick and body contact. As such, infringement of the rules will inevitably occur. In most cases, players who infringe the rules are penalized by having free-hits awarded against them.

Free-hits must be taken on the spot where the infringement occurred except when the offence has been caused by an attacking player in the opposing circle. In this case the defending team can take the free-hit from any spot within that circle or from a spot no more than 16yd (14.5m) from the back-line and exactly in line with the spot where the infringement took place. The ball must be stationary when the free-hit is taken and the striker can push or hit it. The ball must not, however, be raised intentionally or in such a way as to be dangerous in itself, or likely to lead to dangerous play. No players from the opposing team are allowed within 5yd (4.5m) of the ball when the free-hit is taken. When the free-hit to an attacking side is within 5yd (4.5m) of the opposing circle then the players of both teams, except the person taking the free-hit, must be 5yd (4.5m) from the ball. In all cases, the person taking the free-hit must not touch the ball again or remain or approach within playing distance of it until another player from either team has played or touched it.

When an offence is committed by a player in his/her own defensive circle the umpire usually awards a penalty corner against the defending team. Penalty corners can even be awarded against a team if one of its players commits a deliberate foul outside the circle but within their own 25yd (22m) area.

Penalty corners are unique to hockey. When awarded against a team, no more than five of that team are allowed to take up positions behind the goal-line to defend against the penalty corner. The other six defending players are required to retreat beyond the halfway-line. No defender is allowed to cross the goal-line or centre-line until the ball is hit or pushed into play. The umpire has the right to order the penalty corner to be taken again if a defender crosses the goal-line or centre-line before the ball is hit. This power is, of course, used with discretion, and the corner is often allowed to proceed if, in the umpire's opinion, it is clear that the attacking team have not suffered any disadvantage.

A player of the attacking team who takes the corner is allowed to push or hit the ball from a spot on the goal-line not less than 10yd (9m) from the nearest goal post. This hit or push can be taken from whichever side of the goal the attacking team prefers. The player concerned is not required to be wholly inside or outside the field of play when taking the corner.

No attacker is allowed to enter the circle until the ball has been hit or pushed. Furthermore, no player is allowed within 5yd (4.5m) of the ball at the moment it is hit or pushed.

The player taking the corner from the goal-line cannot score a goal directly from the push or hit, even if the ball is deflected into the goal by a defender. The ball must be passed to another player in the attacking team before a shot at goal can be made. In order for a goal to be scored the shot must be made by an attacker from within the circle. Of course, no shot at goal can be made from a penalty corner until the ball is stopped outside the circle. If the first shot at goal is *hit*, the ball is not allowed to cross the goal-line at a height greater than the back or sideboards, i.e. 18in (45cm), unless it has been deflected by the stick or body of a

defender. There is no limit to the height of the push, flick or scoop or any subsequent stroke or shot, subject always to there being no danger to other players.

For any breach of the rules at a penalty corner by the attacking side the umpire may award a free-hit to the defending team. Breaches of the rules by the defending team can result in the corner being re-taken. Persistent breaches may even lead to a penalty stroke being awarded against the defending team.

Penalty strokes are usually awarded to meet offences which may materially affect the outcome of the game, e.g. an accidental kick of the ball which prevents a certain goal, and for deliberate offences within the circle which warrant a more severe penalty than a penalty corner.

The penalty stroke is taken from a spot 7yd (6.5m) in front of the centre of the goal. The member of the attacking team who takes it is allowed to push, flick or scoop the ball at goal. The stroke is usually defended by the goalkeeper of the defending team but if he/she is incapacitated or suspended from play then the team captain can nominate another player to defend against the penalty stroke. This player is entitled to the same privileges of a goalkeeper including the wearing of protective clothing.

During the penalty stroke all the other players of both teams must go beyond the nearer 25yd (22m) line, and are not allowed to influence or attempt to influence the conduct of the penalty stroke.

When taking the penalty stroke the attacker is permitted to take one stride forward and is allowed to raise the ball to any height. The attacker is only permitted to touch the ball once and is not allowed to approach the ball or the goalkeeper after the stroke has been taken.

The goalkeeper is required to stand on the goal-line and is not allowed to leave the goal-line or move either of his/her feet until the ball is played.

Any deliberate action, 'dummy' or feint by the striker to induce the goalkeeper to move prior to the stroke being taken will result in the striker being penalized.

If a goal is scored, the game is restarted with a pass-back from the centre-line. If a goal is not scored, either because the penalty stroke is saved by the goalkeeper or the goal is missed by the stiker, the penalty stroke is ended. The game is restarted by a free-hit taken by a defender from a spot in front of the centre of the goal and at the top of the circle, 16yd (14.5m) from the goal-line.

16-yard hits are equivalent to 'goal-kicks' in soccer. They are awarded to the defending side after the ball has been played over the goal-line by a member of the attacking team. The hit is taken from a spot exactly opposite where it crossed the goal-line and not more than 16yd (14.5m) from that line.

Long corners are awarded to the attacking team when the ball is played unintentionally over the goal-line by a member of the defending team. The ensuing hit is taken by the attacking team from a spot on the goal-line within 5yd (4.5m) of the corner flag.

Push-ins/hit-ins are used to restart the game after the ball has been put out of play over the side-line by one of the players on the pitch. A member of the team that was not responsible for putting the ball out of play is allowed to push or hit the ball into play at the point at which the ball went out. Players from the opposing team must be at least 5yd (4.5m) from the ball at the moment the ball is pushed or hit in.

The bully is also unique to hockey and is only used to restart the game after a simultaneous breach of the rules by members of both teams or if the game has been stopped because of an accident on the field of play or an injury to a player. To perform the bully, a player from each team is required to stand square on to his/her opponent, facing the side-line and with his/her own goal-lines to his/her right. The ball is placed on the ground between the two players and after tapping the ground and each other's sticks alternately three times, the ball can be played. Until the ball is in play no player from either team, except those involved in the bully, should be within 5yd (4.5m) of the ball. Players are no longer required to be 'on-side' at the bully.

Off-side   A player can only be off-side if he/she is in the opposing 25yd (22m) area and is ahead of the ball with fewer than two opponents between himself/herself and the back-line the moment that the ball is played. A player who is behind the ball or in possession of the ball cannot be off-side.

All these rules and guidelines are intended to make hockey a fast, skilful game in which the players compete strongly but fairly and always within the rules. Rough, dangerous play and misconduct in hockey can, in addition to the appropriate penalty, lead to a warning by the umpire. This is indicated by the showing of a green card to the player. More serious and persistent offences of this nature can lead to a player being shown the yellow card and temporarily suspended from the game. The showing of a red card indicates that a player has been sent off and can take no further part in the game.

Good hockey players always try to play the game hard but never in a reckless or dangerous manner, placing skill and fair play above all else.

Vicky Dickson (7) representing England.

RULES
CLINIC

In attempting to intercept a pass a defender in the circle accidentally kicks the ball. What decision should the umpire give?

Award a penalty corner to the attacking side, if in the umpire's opinion there was an unintentional breach of the rules inside the circle by the defending player.

An attacker is in the process of shooting at goal when he/she is unfairly and

Intentionally prevented from doing so by a member of the defending team. What decision should the umpire give?

Award a penalty stroke. If in the umpire's opinion there has been an intentional breach of the rules inside the circle by the player of the defending team then a penalty stroke should be awarded to the attacking team.

In attempting to prevent the ball from entering his/her goal the goalkeeper sweeps the ball out with his/her hand. What should happen next?

The umpire should award a penalty stroke. The goalkeeper is not allowed to strike at the ball with his/her hand or thrust it away with the body.

At the pass-back for the start of play all the players from both teams should be in their own half of the pitch. At the moment the ball is struck the player taking the pass-back is found to be standing in his/her opponent's half. Is this an offence?

No. The rule states quite clearly that all players of both teams *other than the player making the pass-back* must be in their own half of the pitch.

Having played the ball can the player who took the pass-back remain close to it?

No. After making the pass-back the striker of the ball is not allowed to approach within playing distance until it has been touched or played by another member of either team.

What constitutes the offence of obstruction?

It applies to those occasions when a player interposes his/her body or stick as an obstruction between an opposing player and the ball in a manner which prevents the opponent from playing or having an opportunity to play the ball.

Can a player other than the player in possession of the ball be penalized for obstruction?

Yes. It is an offence for a player to interpose himself or herself between an opponent and the ball so that a fellow player can gain a 'clear' advantage when playing the ball. This is known as 'third party interference'.

Is it an offence if the ball strikes the foot or body of a player?

Yes. A player is not allowed to stop, propel, or deflect the ball with any part of his/her body. However, if the ball is propelled straight at a player from close quarters by an opponent and the ball rebounds off him/her then no offence will be considered to have been committed.

A shot by an attacker outside the circle is deflected into the goal by a defender positioned inside the circle. What should the umpire's decision be?

The umpire should award a long corner to the attacking side. For a goal to be scored the ball must be inside the circle when hit by an attacker.

A sliding save by the goalkeeper results in the ball becoming accidentally lodged in his/her legguards. What action should the umpire take?

The umpire should award a 'bully' on a spot in line with where the stoppage of play took place and 16yd (14.5m) from the goal-line or back-line.

Do the players from either team have to be on-side at the time of the 'bully'?

No. There is no requirement for the players to be nearer their own back-line or goal-line than the ball. The only requirement for players not involved in the 'bully' is that they should not be within 5yd (4.5m) of the ball until it is in play.

When is a player considered to be off-side?

If, at the moment the ball is played, he/she is in front of the ball in his/her opponents' 25yd (22m) area, and there are fewer than two opponents between him/her and the opposition goal-line or back-line.

If a player is on-side when the ball is played, but receives the ball in an off-side position, is he/she off-side?

No. A player cannot be judged to be off-side at the moment he/she receives the ball. The umpire can only decide if a player is on-side or off-side at the moment the ball is played.

Can a player be off-side in his/her own half?

No. The only area a player can be off-side is in the opponents' 25yd (22m) area.

At a penalty corner the ball is stopped and then hit fiercely by an attacker into the roof of the goal. Is it a goal?

No. If at a penalty corner the first shot at goal is a hit it must not cross the goal-line at a height higher than the backboards or sideboards i.e. 18in (45cm) unless it is deflected by the stick or body of a defender. The player raising the ball should be penalized for dangerous play and a free-hit awarded to the defending team.

No leeway is given in this clash between Germany and Great Britain.

At a penalty corner the ball is passed rapidly from attacker to attacker, two or three times, without being stopped, after which the ball is hit into the goal. Is it a goal?

No. The rule states quite clearly that no shot at goal can be made from a penalty corner until the ball is stopped, or comes to a stop, or touches the stick or person of a defender.

In attempting to clear the ball from the circle the goalkeeper kicks at and raises it in a manner that causes other players in the circle to take avoiding action. What action should the umpire take?

If in the umpire's opinion the action was unintentional, and no advantage could be gained by the attacking side, a penalty corner should be awarded against the goalkeeper's team on the grounds that the ball was propelled in a way that could be dangerous or lead to dangerous play. If the umpire considered the goalkeeper's action to be intentional, then a penalty stroke should be awarded to the attacking team.

In the game of hockey, what constitutes misconduct?

Rough or dangerous play, time wasting, deliberate breach of any rule, or any other behaviour which in the umpire's opinion is detrimental to the game can be considered to be misconduct. The awardable penalties are limited primarily to:

1 a free hit
2 a penalty corner
3 a penalty stroke

but can be expanded to a warning (green card), a temporary suspension (yellow card), or suspension for the remainder of the game (red card). An umpire is entitled to use any of these separately or in conjunction with one of the three primary penalties.

TECHNIQUE

At first sight hockey can appear a technically difficult game. Much of this difficulty is attributed to the fact that the exponents are required to control a ball $4\frac{1}{2}$in (11.4cm) in diameter with an implement 36–40in (91–101cm) long but no more than 2in (5cm) wide at its widest point. Add to this uneven playing surfaces, poor weather conditions and two teams who through legitimate tactical ploys endeavour to make the game as difficult as possible for each other, and you have an almost impossible situation to cope with. New designs in equipment, advanced technology, the advent of artifical playing surfaces and better coaching have all contributed to making the game a great deal easier and more enjoyable to play and watch.

But perhaps the most important factor in all this is the competence of the individual players themselves. This is determined by a player's own mastery of the basic skills and understanding of the fundamentals of the game.

The problem of mastery and effective implementation of skills confounds both the beginner and the advanced player. Competence at the basic skills is a framework upon which one's performance in the game is built. All hockey skills consist of three essential integrated sequences:

1 Receiving.
2 Controlling.
3 Passing.

There are, within these, a number of other elements:

Tackling, intercepting, dribbling, running with the ball, shooting and the actual game situations which arise when these sequences are linked together. The skill of the players is an essential factor in determining the amount of time the ball remains in play. The more skilful the players the longer the ball will be in play – or the longer and more expansive will be the playing sequences. The obvious conclusion to be drawn from this is that it is very important to develop as high a level of skill as possible in order to maximize the amount of time that one's own team has the ball, increasing the opportunities to create and score goals.

Passing

Passing is the building block of team play. Many coaches say, 'If you can't pass you can't play.' So if a group of players want to be successful as a team they must learn to pass accurately to each other.

A pass involves two players – the passer and receiver – but includes a number of other elements which influence and affect the outcome of the pass. Anyone who has watched a game of hockey will be only too aware of the astonishingly high number of passes that go astray. In fact, in matches played at lower levels the best way to get the ball to another member of one's own team is to give it to the opposition who invariably give it straight back. Those people who have played the game appreciate that making successful passes is not as easy as it looks,

HOCKEY

especially when one considers the number of factors that have to be taken into consideration when attempting to make a pass in hockey.

The player must bear in mind that the aim of the player with the ball is for his team to retain possession until an opportunity arises to launch an attack on the opposition circle and goal. Effective passing depends on a number of simple but fundamental principles:

1 The player must have control of the ball.
2 The player must be balanced.
3 The player must be aware of the position of his/her team-mates and his/her opponents.

This is the ABC of passing and this, together with the ability to know when to pass and when to hold the ball, all adds up to 'reading the game'. But even players blessed with 'vision' have to practise passing constantly.

Generally speaking, there are five types of pass which need to be practised and used.

The push pass This is the most common way of passing and although it does not generate the same ball speed as a hit it is the most effective and accurate of all techniques.

The hands should be held comfortably apart on the stick with the left hand at the top and the right hand approximately a third to half way down the shaft of the stick. Lowering the right hand will help to give greater control. Both hands should grasp the stick firmly.

The body should be crouched with knees bent. The left foot and shoulder should point in the direction that the ball is to travel. The

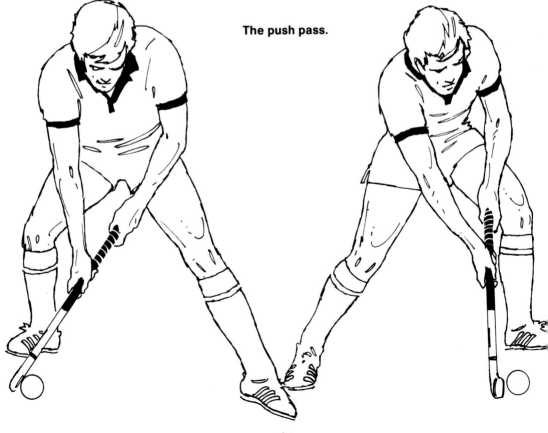

The push pass.

The grip for the push pass showing clearly the left hand gripping the top of the stick while the right hand is positioned about a third to half way down the shaft.

Note how the stick stays in contact with the ball and how the body weight is transferred from the right to the left leg.

The reverse stick push.

Note how the ball is released close to the right foot and that the power for the pass is generated by the right hand. The grip for the reverse stick push clearly shows the position of the hands on the stick.

player's head should be kept over or in line with the path of the ball. The body weight should be transferred from the right foot to the left foot as the pass is made. The face of the stick should be kept in contact with the ground and ball throughout the movement. It should be angled towards the ground to prevent the ball bouncing upwards.

The reverse stick push   The techniques used are similar to those of the push pass, except that it is executed from the reverse stick position and the toe of the stick is used – see drawing above. This pass is often played to add a degree of deception to a move and is often an extension of a dribble or subtle 'dummy' move.

The slap   This is used almost as often as the push pass. The techniques involved are similar, but while the push pass is most effective over short distances, the slap is used to make long, powerful, penetrative passes. The additional impetus is imparted to the ball by drawing the stick away from the ball and then making contact with the ball in a 'sweeping' action. The stick head is usually in constant contact with the ground. To make a more powerful pass the stick head can be drawn back and raised behind the player's body as in the hit. The right and left hands remain apart as for the push pass.

The slap.

Note the distance of the stick from the ball at the start of the movement and, once again, how power is added to the pass by transferring the body weight from the right to the left leg.

The hit.

Note how the player steps into the stroke with his left leg and shoulder pointing in the direction of the hit.

The grip for the hit.

The hit Players use the hit to propel the ball quickly over relatively long distances. It is also used to make penetrating passes through opposition lines as in crosses into the circle, at free-hits and for shots at goal. In each of these situations the player will be required to strike the ball accurately, smoothly and hard either when it is stationary or moving. In many cases the player and ball will be moving together, sometimes at top speed, so increasing the degree of difficulty involved in executing the stroke.

Unlike the push and the slap the stick is held with both hands, left hand above the right, at the top of the stick. But as with all passing skills it is important that the leading shoulder, in this case the left one, is pointing in the direction of the pass.

The stick is drawn back behind the right

Ties Kruize of the Netherlands, considered by many to be the most complete player of his time.

shoulder and then swept forward in a swinging action to strike the ball level with the left foot. The arms are usually straight at the point of impact. The follow-through should follow the direction of the pass.

More power and therefore greater ball speed can be generated by transferring the body weight from the right to the left leg, both of which will be slightly bent but braced at the time of impact. Some players utilize a whipping wrist action to generate more power from the stroke while others still use a rotation of the upper body to assist them.

Generally speaking, the ball will be struck while positioned by the left foot but there are many occasions in the game when the player will not have time or space to adopt the ideal position and will therefore need to strike the ball when it is by or even behind his/her right foot. This too needs to be practised.

The flick   This is essentially an overhead or aerial pass which is used to drop the ball in space behind the opposition defence. It can be played from a stationary position or on the move. Skillful players can propel the ball for 50yd (45m) or more. The grip and body position are similar to those used for the push. The ball, however, needs to be positioned well in front of the left foot with the stick head placed under the ball and the stick face angled upwards. The body should be crouched with the knees bent and the body weight slightly over the right leg.

In executing the pass the body weight is transferred from the right to the left foot while the arms and stick attempt to lift the ball upwards and forwards. The follow-through and moment of release will determine the trajectory of the ball. Additional power and distance can be generated through and by the right leg.

The flick.

Receiving the ball

In any team game in which passing is involved it is essential for players to be able to receive and control a ball whenever or wherever it comes from, whether under pressure or in space. No matter how talented a player is, he/she will be of little use to the team if their ability to receive and control a pass is poor.

There are a few occasions when a player receiving a ball will need to stop it 'dead'. Generally speaking, however, the receiver of a pass will be required to bring the ball under control and reposition it in preparation for the next move, whether it be a pass, dribble or shot. A player must learn to perform this skill in minimum time and with maximum effect.

The principles which underlie the execution of this skill are the same whether the ball is approaching from in front of or behind the player or whether from the left or right.

Receiving while stationary The left hand should grip the stick at the top while the right hand is placed about one-third to halfway down the shaft. The stick should be held upright with the shaft and face inclined towards the ground so that the ball does not rebound upwards.

Whenever possible the players' head and body should be brought into line with the path of the ball and the ball watched onto the stick. To cushion the impact and effect greater control it may sometimes be necessary to allow the right hand and stick to 'give' a little at the moment of contact.

Generally speaking, the ball is controlled next to the right foot when receiving on the open-stick side and next to the left foot when receiving on the reverse-stick side. The ball can also be received with the open stick when it is near the left foot.

Note how the ball is positioned well in front of the left foot at the moment of contact so allowing the face of the stick to be placed under the ball in order to lift and direct it upwards. The right leg is bent at the point stick and ball make contact in order to generate power into the shot. The follow through and point of release determines the height and path through which the ball will travel.

HOCKEY

When playing on artificial grass or indoors, it is possible to use a 'flat' stick to receive the ball on either the open or reverse stick side. Once again it is important to make sure that the face of the stick is inclined towards the ground in order to 'trap' the ball when it arrives. Receiving with a flat stick will allow the player to take the ball further away from his/her feet.

Receiving with an upright stick and receiving with a flat stick. In both instances note that the grip is similar, the ball is received close to the right foot and the stick face is angled towards the ground in order to trap the ball.

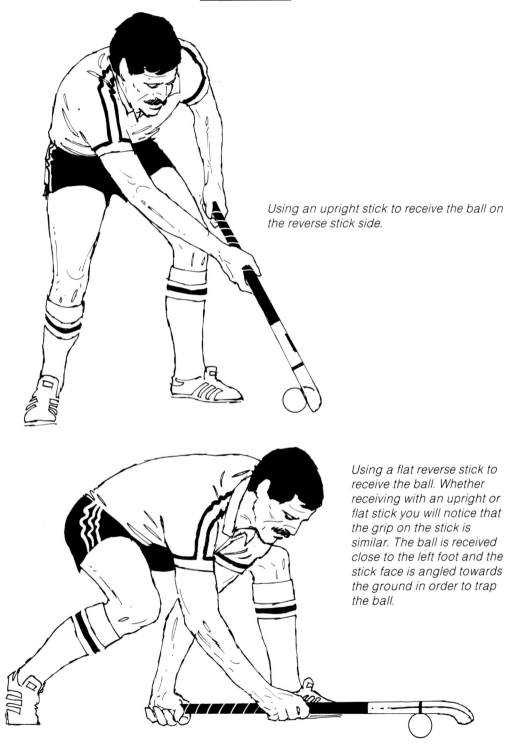

Using an upright stick to receive the ball on the reverse stick side.

Using a flat reverse stick to receive the ball. Whether receiving with an upright or flat stick you will notice that the grip on the stick is similar. The ball is received close to the left foot and the stick face is angled towards the ground in order to trap the ball.

The aerial trap.

The player keeps her eyes on the ball and the stick is kept below shoulder level as she moves into line with the ball.

The ball is played downwards so that it lands close to the right foot.

The angled stick is used to add that final control to the movement. Note the stick and body position at this point.

Receiving an aerial pass In the modern game players are often called upon to receive and control aerial passes. The first requirement is that the ball must be below shoulder height when it is played with the stick. The stick should be held as for the push pass with the left hand at the top and the right hand one-third or halfway down the stick. The shaft and the face of the stick should be angled so as to allow the ball to be deflected downwards. It should be brought under control near to the player's feet. The stick may then be used to trap the ball before executing the next move.

Running with and without the ball

The modern game demands that the very best players are also good athletes. Although there is no need for good hockey players to be 'even time' sprinters with the stamina of marathon runners, it is essential for modern hockey players to be fit and able to run effectively, efficiently and well. As with all other techniques this requires practice and should include running backwards, sideways and forwards and vary from jogging through striding to sprinting.

Running with the ball encompasses a number of techniques and requires the player to 'carry' or propel the ball with the stick without any exaggerated or complex movement of the ball. As such this will allow them to look up and assess the situation before choosing the next move.

Running with the ball is most effective

Running with the ball.

Note how the stick and ball are held in front of and to the right of the player's body. The stick is in constant contact with the ball.

Running with the ball and 'scanning'.

Note how the position of the stick and ball allows the player to look up and ahead to see what options are available to her.

Dribbling and dodging

While it is accepted that passing is the most effective way of beating an opponent it is sometimes necessary to use the individual skills of dribbling or dodging to evade an opponent and set up an attack.

Players who can beat opponents by dribbling or dodging have the ability to create the 'extra player' for their team in attacking situations as well as being equipped to get their team and themselves out of difficult and sometimes dangerous situations in defence.

Players who dribble and dodge always run the risk of being dispossessed. Developing the right attitude to the chances of success and failure when dribbling is an important part of this skill. Players should become aware of the importance of this skill and the conditions under which it should be performed.

For easy, fluid control the stick should be held at the top by the left hand with the right hand one-third to halfway down the shaft. Allowance should be made for individual preference.

It is the left hand which controls the twisting, rotational movement of the stick while the right hand generates the pulling and pushing action necessary for moving the ball. The right hand also provides the control and stability for the action. The ball is tapped or dragged from left to right with a rolling action of the wrists. This skill is often described as the Indian dribble. Once mastered it can be developed and extended to include the skills of feinting and dodging.

The feint or dodge is made by combining and co-ordinating the movements of body,

when there is plenty of time and space to operate in and there are no opponents in close proximity. In this situation there is usually no need to dribble past or beat an opponent.

In order to run effectively with the ball it is necessary to hold the body as near upright as possible, holding the stick at the top with the left hand. The right hand is also held much higher up the shaft and near to the left hand. The stick and ball should be keep well out in front of the body and slightly to the right, so making it easier to run at speed and to look up while doing so.

Good balanced footwork is essential, as is the ability to 'scan' ahead to read the pattern of play. Players must learn to recognize when they should dribble and when they should run with the ball. Both skills require close control.

TECHNIQUE

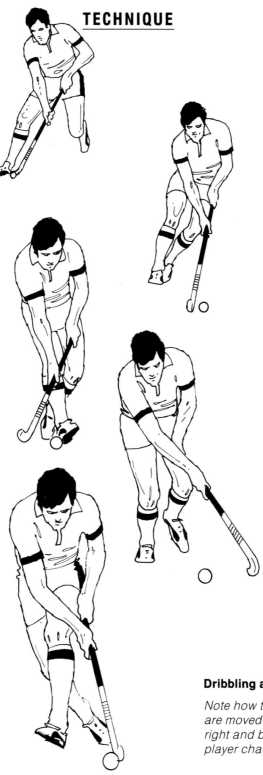

Dribbling and dodging.

Note how the body, stick and ball are moved smoothly from left to right and back again as the player changes direction.

Dribbling and dodging.

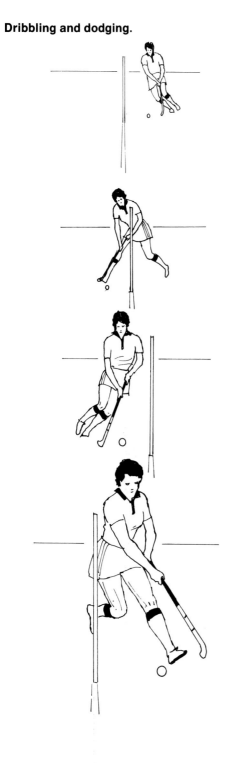

stick and ball. The object at all times is to give the impression that you are moving in one direction, then suddenly, when your opponent is committed to covering your first move, you change direction and move past the opponent on the other side.

Players on the right side of the pitch may look to beat their opponents on the open-stick side. As the defender moves his body weight or stick to the right to cover the move the attacker changes the point of his attack to the defender's reverse-stick side, dragging the ball from left to right, and dribbling past the defender at speed.

Similarly, players on the left side of the pitch can deceive defenders into believing they want to beat them on their reverse-stick side. When the defender moves to cover this threat the attacker switches the point of attack from the defender's reverse-stick to the open-stick side. The ball is dragged from right to left at speed and under close control.

TECHNIQUE

Dribbling and dodging in action.

The player in the dark shirt evades the tackle of an opposing player by using dribbling and dodging skills of the highest order. Close control and exceptional balance are essential in these situations.

A player moving at pace, making it difficult for the defender.

An interception made with the reverse stick.

The defending player foils an attack by the opposing team by making a superb interception using the flat, reverse stick technique.

Winning the ball

When a team is in possession of the ball their main aim is to keep possession for long enough to launch an attack and score a goal. The defending team aim to prevent them from doing this. They also intend to gain possession of the ball in order to initiate their own attack on the opposition goal.

The defending team can win possession of the ball by intercepting poor or badly timed passes and by tackling the attacking player while he/she is still in possession of the ball.

Intercepting This does away with the need for tackling and often results in clean, quality control of the ball from which quick, effective counter-attacks can be launched. It requires the ability to mark well, read the game and anticipate what opponents are going to do next.

If an interception cannot be made, it may be necessary for the defender to reposition him/her self so he/she can channel, shadow and close the attacker down with the ultimate intention of dispossessing him with a tackle.

Tackling Good hockey teams use tackling as the launching pad for creative, attacking play. While the ultimate aim is to regain possession of the ball, tackling, like intercepting can be used to put the ball out of play so allowing the defending team time to reform.

It is important for the defender to watch the ball and react to it and not to the movements of stick or body of the player in possession. Secondly, the defender must learn to time the tackle correctly and not be tempted to 'dive in' at the wrong time. Thirdly, players must recognize when to tackle and which tackle to use. While most players will need to use only one or two types of tackle most of the time, it is important for all players to be able to execute all types of tackle.

Whenever possible, the tackler should shepherd the attacker on to his/her open-stick or 'wrong' side. This requires good balanced foot and leg work, often in a crouched position.

The jab tackle   The success of this tackle depends on its speed of execution and directness. The stick is held in the left hand and is lunged at the ball, very much like the head of a striking snake. The tackler moves like a fencer, leading with the left foot but making sure that he/she is not over-committed or put off-balance. Sufficient control must be retained to recover and tackle again if the first tackle is not successful.

The jab tackle can be used as a decoy to set up a secondary tackle. It can be used to force the attacker to lose control of the ball and subsequently slow the attack down. It can be used to put the ball out of play or it can be used to propel the ball away from the attacker and towards the tackler's own team-mates.

The jab tackle.

Note the balanced position of the defender and the way in which the stick is used to jab at and dispossess the attacker.

The defending player's entire concentration is centred on the ball as he prepares to make a tackle. The position of his stick and feet indicate that he will attempt a jab tackle.

The open-stick tackle.

Good defenders usually adopt a boxer's or fencer's stance with one foot in advance of the other. The rear foot is often used as a pivot or driving force to effect the tackle.

The open-stick tackle Sometimes known as the block tackle, this is the most common way of dispossessing an attacker. It is performed over a wide range and at varying angles. It can be performed while stationary or on the move.

The tackle is sometimes preceded by a 'dummy' jab tackle and is performed by using the stick as a barrier either close to the defender's own feet or wide on the defender's open-stick side. As with the jab tackle, this tackle requires good timing, footwork and balance. The left foot once again leads the action. The right foot acts as a pivot in the event of a failed attempt or need to change direction.

When performed on the move it is important that the defender positions himself goalside and to the right of the attacker before attempting to tackle.

The block tackle.

The defender adopts a strong, well-balanced position as he makes his tackle on the attacker.

TECHNIQUE

The reverse-stick tackle.

The reverse-stick tackle   The need to be goalside is never more important than when making this tackle. As both body and stick contact is forbidden by the rules it is imperative that the defender gets into a position which allows him/her to make the tackle level with or ahead of his/her own body.

Although it is recommended that two hands be used when tackling, it may be necessary to tackle one-handed when tackling wide of the body. The further away from the feet that the tackle is made, the flatter the stick must be to the ground. Tackles with flat sticks are more common and effective when playing on artificial surfaces or indoors.

Note how the shaft of the stick is laid flat with the face angled towards the ground.

A defender attempting to make a reverse-stick tackle. Note the strong position in which the attacker has the ball – well out in front of his body and on his open stick side.

The goalkeeper usually uses his left hand to save high shots at goal.

Goalkeeping

By definition alone the goalkeeper's role in the team is to protect the goal and keep it intact. In modern hockey, both indoor and outdoor, the goalkeeper is also expected to dominate and control what happens in the circle physically, vocally and psychologically.

Hockey goalkeeping is a highly specialized position and anyone choosing to play in goal must not only have a physical presence but also speed, strength, stamina, agility, flexibility, courage and confidence.

As with all other aspects of hockey, training and practise are essential and care and attention must always be paid to the specialized needs of the position.

Goalkeeping has been described as a position of highs and lows – 'depending on where the shots at goal are placed'. The majority of shots will be placed along or near the ground, in which case the ball should be played using the stick or pads and kickers, whichever is appropriate and most effective at the time. Shots in the air will be saved with the body, arms and hands.

In all these situations the goalkeeper's action will start from the accepted position of balanced readiness. The goalkeeper can use this position as a springboard for any move or save that is required. Whichever technique is selected the fundamental requirements of good goalkeeping remain the same:

TECHNIQUE

Spectacular use of the body and arms in an attempt to make a save.

1 Good balance.
2 Good anticipation.
3 Good reflexes.
4 Good footwork.
5 Head and body in line with the path of the ball.
6 Eyes on the ball.

Low shots directed straight at the goalkeeper should be stopped with the pads. Bringing the legs together will present a wider barrier. The impact of the shot can be absorbed and the rebound controlled by bending the knees slightly on contact. The ball should then be cleared using the stick or foot. It is important for the ball to be cleared towards the sidelines, never back into the middle of the circle. Modern goalkeeping often requires a goalkeeper to use the 'save-clear' method of defending the goal and circle. This technique obviates the need to stop the ball and either the right or left leg is used to save and clear the ball to safety in one action. Good technique is essential. The head should be over the ball as the kick is made with the body weight being propelled through the ball. The ball should be kicked along the ground. If the goalkeeper has to stretch or lean backwards, the chances are that the ball will rise up dangerously and the action will be penalized.

Obviously there are times when the goalkeeper will be required to make saves using the stick or hand. Usually the ball will be in the air in which case the hand should

TECHNIQUE

The goalkeeper slides, right leg forward, in an attempt to dispossess the attacker. Note how the stick is also ready for use if needed.

be used to provide as large a barrier as possible. If, however, the ball is placed beyond the reach of the goalkeeper's hands, the stick can be used.

As with the use of the pads, the hand is used to cushion and control the shot. The ball must not be held. As the ball falls to the ground it must be cleared in a controlled fashion using stick or pads.

Diving saves, to left or right, are made in a similar fashion to soccer goalkeepers, with the appropriate hand being brought over and across to play the ball. As most hockey goalkeepers hold the stick in the right hand, it is usual for only the left hand to be used to make high saves. Today's rules, however, allow goalkeepers to use their sticks when

The Egyptian goalkeeper spreading himself at the feet of an advancing attacker.

making saves above shoulder height.

The stick is invariably used in making low diving saves to the goalkeeper's right. In developing these skills goalkeepers and their coaches must continue to give attention to good balanced footwork. It is this that gets a goalkeeper into position to make the save. Although the attacker has the initial advantage because he/she has the ball and is in a position to decide where, when and how to shoot, the goalkeeper can work to make the attacker's job more difficult by reducing or narrowing the angles available to the attacker.

By staying on the goal-line, the goalkeeper offers the striker large target areas to aim at. By moving towards the attacker, the goalkeeper will narrow and close the angles so reducing the target areas – until eventually the target will be completely blocked from the attacker's view,

The kick save.

This goalkeeper has got to the ball and cleared it with a safe kick.

Whenever possible goalkeepers will use their pads and kickers to make saves.

A goalkeeper about to kick clear.

which may force him/her to shoot straight at the goalkeeper or high and wide of the target.

It is important for goalkeepers to assess correctly when and how to come off their lines. In doing so, it is essential for the goalkeeper to stay on his or her feet for as long as possible in readiness to move or dive sideways to block the ball, as and when the attacker tries to go round the goalkeeper.

Going down too early can leave a goalkeeper stranded and also vulnerable to the lofted or chipped shot.

Finally, all good goalkeepers must know how to command the circle both physically and vocally. They should not be afraid of marshalling the defence and they should always look to be not only the last line of defence but also the 'launching pad' of many attacks.

Diving saves to left and right require the left hand to be used wherever possible. Today's rules permit the stick to be used above shoulder height.

The goalkeeper has used a very difficult technique, the reverse-stick tackle, to prevent the attacking player from getting around him.

HOCKEY

Shooting

Goalscoring is arguably the most important aspect of hockey. All players like to and enjoy scoring spectacular goals. The reality of the situation is that all goals are good goals and leading goal scorers in any game will confirm that they are looking to pick up as many, if not more, 'bread and butter' goals as spectacular ones.

Good strikers not only know how to shoot, but also where to shoot from and what to aim at. They work to realize the 'position of maximum opportunity'.

Rick Charlesworth, Australian hockey star, demonstrating total commitment to the game.

Arguably the most important aspect of shooting and goalscoring is the will or desire to shoot. Uncharitable though it may sound, it is not unfair to say that leading goalscorers in a team tend to be a little selfish. They believe, quite correctly, that if they do not seize on every opportunity and half-chance, it is unlikely that they will score many goals. They, nevertheless, have to learn when it is impossible to score, at which point they must look to pass to someone in a more favourable position.

It goes without saying that all shots at goal should be on target. Shots that go high or wide are a waste of effort. Shots on target, if saved by the goalkeeper or defender, often rebound and lead to secondary strike opportunities. The importance and wisdom of following up all shots – whether your own or that of a colleague – must be stressed. In most goalscoring opportunities, as with knock-downs and rebounds, the ball will often arrive awkwardly. Strikers have to chase fifty-fifty balls, intercept crosses, pick up deflections and collect passes which arrive at different heights and then, whether marked or unmarked, have to control the ball, and select the appropriate shooting technique in order to make a shot at goal. The higher the level of play, the less time will be available to them.

Good technique and powers of concentration allow strikers to take greater advantage of the half-chances that come their way. The real key to being a top goalscorer is the desire and determination to have a go and the courage and commitment to take responsibility for your actions.

Restarts and set plays

Every game of hockey contains a large number of stoppages. Restarts and set plays are an essential and integral part of the

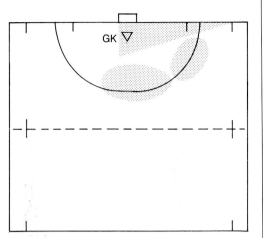

Long corners.

Attacking teams must look to exploit the danger areas in the opposition circle at long corners. These are shown as the shaded areas in this diagram.

game and, as such should be understood, rehearsed and perfected in order to get maximum advantage from them.

The most common situations from which restarts and set plays are:

1 Free-hits.
2 Hit-ins from the side-line.
3 Long corners.
4 Penalty corners.

Other restarts such as the push-back and bully have been referred to elsewhere in this book.

In every situation, the attacking team will be endeavouring to maximize their goal-scoring opportunities, while the defending side will be working to deny them. Each will be seeking to wrest the initiative from the other.

Free-hits In order to get the most advantage from a free-hit, the team in

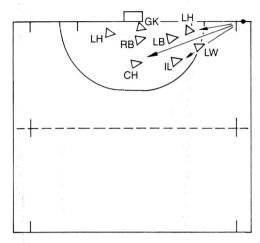

When defending against a long corner it is important to position players in areas that prevent the opposition from exploiting the danger areas.

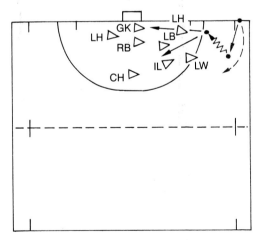

The defending players must also be prepared to counter any variations, such as the 'short' long corner, that the attacking team might try to use.

possession should attempt to take it as quickly as possible and certainly before the defending team has had time to reorganize. This demands split-second timing and high levels of concentration. Every member of the team must be aware of what is going on and be prepared to act or react as required.

There is a huge difference between taking a quick free-hit and taking it too quickly. All too often, players feel under pressure to keep the momentum of the attack going or to 'get the ball up the other end'. This invariably leads to a loss of hard-won possession. So if the opportunity for taking an effective quick free-hit is not there, the team in possession must fall back on well known, well drilled, effective free-hits. This will only happen if the objectives of each free-hit are known to all the players in the team. Some common objectives are:

1 Don't speculate, calculate – especially in the defensive zone.
2 Whenever possible, get the ball going forward near or into the danger areas in and around the opposition circle.
3 The player on the ball must decide what happens but it is the players off the ball who, by moving into or creating space, dictate what happens next.
4 Keep possession.

Hit-ins from the side-line   The same principles and objectives apply to these situations, although the opportunity to put the ball into play quickly may not always be possible, except in championship/ international hockey where ball boys and girls are provided.

Since the options available from restarts on or near the side-lines are much smaller in number, it is difficult for truly incisive play to be initiated from these situations. The priority must therefore be to retain possession from the first pass, so creating a launching pad for subsequent attacking moves.

Long corners   Opportunities to take long corners quickly are rare and as such the defending team will have time to reorganize themselves. Remember too that there will usually be more defenders in this area than attackers. Furthermore the circle is always very congested and the marking tight. Time spent on thinking out and rehearsing set-piece moves at long corners is well worth the effort.

The crucial areas to try and exploit are clearly shown in the illustration. The players off the ball should work to create openings for themselves and team-mates in these areas. The attacking players should manoeuvre to receive and control the ball on the open-stick side and in a position that allows them to attack the markers on the reverse-stick side.

For the defending side, the problems will be different if not exactly the opposite. Defending players will be expected to counter every move by the attacking side and prevent the ball being received by the attackers in the danger areas. This calls for as many players as possible being available to help. But a superiority of numbers will not be of much use if they do not work together to take up and cover certain basic positions. The goalkeeper is the key defender and the team defence should always allow the 'keeper to have a clear view of the ball.

Occasionally, attacking teams will try to move a well organized defence by playing the ball short and then working it into the danger areas. Defending sides should be alert to this and the job of closing down the player with the ball should be allocated to specific defenders.

Penalty corners   This aspect of hockey is unique in that the rules of the game place limitations and restrictions on both the attacking and defending sides. These must be taken into consideration when executing attacking moves or defending against them.

Players lining up to defend a penalty corner.

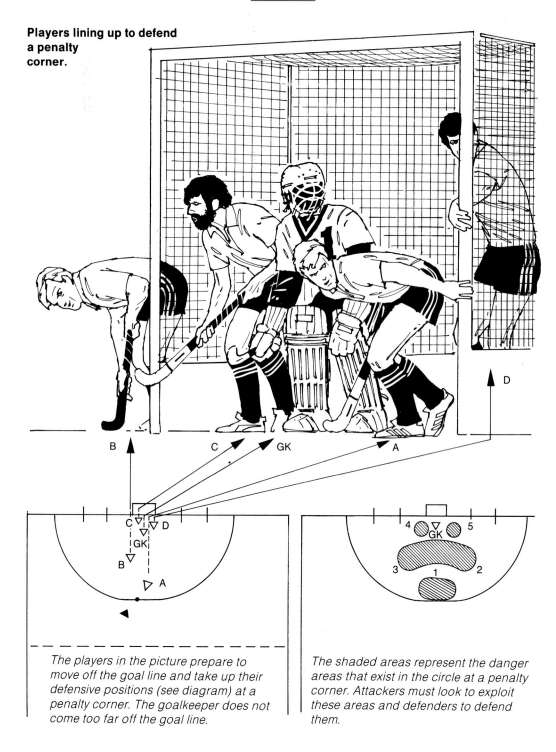

The players in the picture prepare to move off the goal line and take up their defensive positions (see diagram) at a penalty corner. The goalkeeper does not come too far off the goal line.

The shaded areas represent the danger areas that exist in the circle at a penalty corner. Attackers must look to exploit these areas and defenders to defend them.

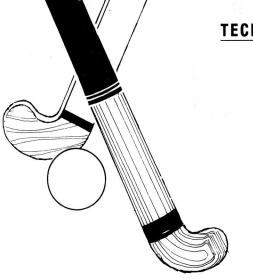

TECHNIQUE

Players C and D each have responsiblity for the areas on either side of the goalkeeper and near to the goal posts.

(c) The goalkeeper usually takes up a position covering the middle parts of the goal but in advance of players C and D. This position may be 2, 3 or even as much as 7yd off the goal-line.

(d) Occasionally player D is deployed in a position alongside and to the left of the goalkeeper from where he/she will be expected to cover any passes into an area to the left of and behind player A.

1 Defending penalty corners

The first limitation is that only four players and the goalkeeper are allowed to defend the penalty corner. No such limitation is placed on the numbers that the attacking team can employ. The first question that the defence must answer is how to deploy five players to cover all the options available to the attack.

One common pattern for defending penalty corners is described below.

(a) Player A runs out to put the striker of the penalty corner under pressure. In so doing, his aim is to hurry the striker into his shot and possibly a mistake and/or to charge down the shot. He/she should take a line that allows him/her to play the ball with the open stick, while covering any possibility of passes into area 2. He/she should also be prepared to slow down if it is obvious they are not going to get the shot or if the ball is passed to another striker. He/she must now be prepared to assist the other members of the defence in repelling subsequent phases of the attack.

(b) Player B runs to the right of player A and slightly behind. It is his/her job to cover and intercept any passes to attackers in and around area 3. He/she may also have the additional responsibility of dealing with rebounds, knock-downs and other secondary phases of defence, whether off the goalkeeper or any other player.

HOCKEY

Defending penalty corners.

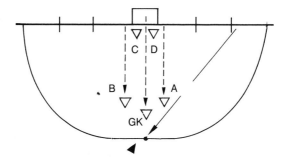

This diagram shows the positions that the defending players must adopt when the goalkeeper comes a long way off the goal line to defend the shot at goal.

Rebounds, knock-downs or deflections off and around the goalkeeper's left will also be his/her responsibility. This move may also help to catch advancing attackers in an off-side position.

(e) Some goalkeepers come as far as possible off their goal-lines in order to narrow the angle of the shot and exert pressure on the striker. Two things need to be borne in mind. Firstly, the closer to the shot the goalkeeper is, the less time he/she has to react to the shot. Secondly, the further off the goal-line they are, the more vulnerable the goal is to shots from wide positions.

As with long corners, the 'keeper is the key defender and must at all times be allowed a clear sight of the ball. He/she alone is equipped to deal effectively and safely with direct shots at goal.

The very best goalkeepers today feel confident enough in their equipment and ability to use their entire bodies to smother and save shots at goal. This is an advanced skill and should not be attempted by the novice goalkeeper. The importance and value of using correct equipment and coaching, particularly with beginners and young players cannot be over stressed.

The entire body can be used to smother and save shots at goal.

Jane Sixsmith, England's swift and skilful striker in action.

Players prepared to shoot at a penalty corner. The diagram shows the options the players can take when shooting at a penalty corner.

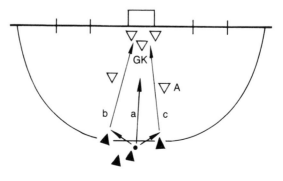

2 Attacking at penalty corners

Attacking at penalty corners is a matter of good team-work, involving individual brilliance as well as collective effort. In theory, with only five defenders to beat, every penalty corner should produce a goal or at least a shot at goal. The statistics indicate that in practice this is not as easy as it might at first appear. Nevertheless, good penalty-corner drills contribute greatly to a team's success. In preparing to be successful at penalty corners it is important to consider the options available.

(a) The first option is to have a direct shot on goal.

(b) If this is not possible, it may be necessary to move the ball over to another area of the circle from which a shot may be made. As there are no restrictions on how many of the attacking team can take part in the penalty corner, it is always possible to employ more players in the move than the defence can cover.

(c) It follows that all moves should look to exploit those areas of the circle which the defenders cannot protect. The attacking team always have the advantage at penalty corners as the defending team can only try to anticipate what is going to happen, so making it difficult to take account of every possibility.

To retain this advantage, the attacking team should have at their disposal a series of set-piece variations to employ according to the situation. The more simple and direct these are the more likely they are to succeed. A few variations are demonstrated in the diagrams.

Many games of hockey, both indoor and outdoor, are decided on the effective execution and defence of penalty corners, especially where two teams are evenly matched. Most top teams today practise and have at their disposal a variety of drills, both in attack and defence, which they can call upon and apply according to the game's needs.

USEFUL
ADDRESSES

International Hockey Federation
Avenue des Arts 1
Box 5
B – 1040 Brussels
Belgium

All England Women's Hockey Association
51 High Street
Shrewsbury
Shropshire
SX1 1ST
Telephone: 0743 233572

All England Women's Hockey Association Coaching Office
2nd Floor
10 Parsonage Street
Dursley
Glos GL11 4EA

The Hockey Association Headquarters
Norfolk House
102 Saxon Gate West
Milton Keynes
MK9 2EP
Telephone: 0908 241100

The Hockey Association Coaching Office
Norfolk House
102 Saxon Gate
Milton Keynes
MK9 2EP
Telephone: 0908 241100

USEFUL · ADDRESSES

The Sports Council
16 Upper Woburn Place
London WC1H 0QP
Telephone: 071 388 1277

The National Coaching Foundation
114 Cardigan Road
Headingley
Leeds
LS6 3BJ
Telephone: 0532 744802

Scottish Hockey Union
48 Pleasance
Edinburgh
EH8 9TJ
Telephone: 031 650 8170

Welsh Women's Hockey Association
Deeside Leisure Centre
Chester Road West
Queensbury
Deeside
Clwyd
CH5 1SA
Telephone: 0244 811825

Irish Hockey Union (Men's)
6a Woodbine Park
Blackrock
Dublin
Irish Republic
Telephone: 010 3531 260 0028

RULES CLINIC

INDEX

**An attacker showing remarkable dribbling
control whilst running at full speed.**

INDEX